Route 66 Po

*Greetings from the
Mother Road*

Michael Wallis & Suzanne Fitzgerald Wallis

St. Martin's Press
New York

Acknowledgments

We are particularly grateful to Katherine Hamilton-Smith, Curator, and Christine A. Pyle, Assistant Curator, at the Lake County Museum, Wauconda, Illinois, for their research assistance and permission to reprint postcard images from the Curt Teich Postcard Archives. We also appreciate the kind assistance and reprint permission of Bettie Fox, National Advertising, Arlington, Texas; and Kim Kaufman, Customer Service, MWM Dexter, Inc., Aurora, Missouri. We also thank the following for their permission to reprint postcard images: Bruce Fincham, Smith-Southwestern, Inc. (for the cover image), Phoenix, Arizona; Carolyn Bastian, Standard Printing Company, Hannibal, Missouri; Winifred Brown, John W. Gough Photo and Postcard Service Collection, Houston, Texas; and Glenn O. Blair, Camdenton, Missouri. We are also grateful to the following individuals for their help in producing this book: Dixie Haas of The Wallis Group, Dorothy Marang, Robert Weil, Jim Fitzgerald, Jaye Zimet, Mara Lurie, Becky Koh, and Twisne Fan.

This book is dedicated to the memory of Jack Rittenhouse.

ROUTE 66 POSTCARDS: GREETINGS FROM THE MOTHER ROAD. Copyright © 1993 by Michael Wallis and Suzanne Fitzgerald Wallis. All rights reserved. No part of this book may be used or reproduced in any manner whatsoever without written permission except in the case of brief quotations embodied in critical articles or reviews. For information, address St. Martin's Press, 175 Fifth Avenue, New York, N. Y. 10010.

ISBN 0-312-09904-5

Printed in Singapore

First Edition: September 1993
10 9 8 7 6 5 4 3 2 1

Dear Fellow Traveler,

The special charm of Route 66—the road of Dust Bowl migrants, GIs headed to battle, wayfaring pilgrims, and legions of tourists—is still going strong. The old road, although varicose and worn in places, continues to draw new generations of dedicated travelers. No matter if they come from Paris, Berlin, London, or Tokyo, no matter if they call New York, Peoria, Little Rock, or Reno their home-town, all Route 66 "road warriors" have one thing in common—they are eager to escape the predictable interstate highways and to find the adventure that awaits on America's Main Street.

Those of us who truly love and appreciate the magic of Route 66—who have heard the music in that ribbon of asphalt and concrete—treasure the myriad of entertaining postcards from the road. Our refrigerator and kitchen cabinets are covered with scores of colorful cards bearing tidings from pals we have met in the eight Route 66 states. Pure slices of Americana, these postcards are a visual shorthand for every journey, east or west, on Route 66. The best of the postcards depict the broad array of edifices, eateries, and honest kitsch that remains along the entire 2,400-plus-mile route. They immortalize hundreds of cafes and greasy spoons, natural and man-made attractions, authentic tourist traps, neon palaces offering a bed for the night, and all the other sights worth writing home about.

Postcards bearing hastily dashed messages and greetings from the road bring a little bit of the vacation experience to the folks who keep the home fires burning, feed the pets, collect the mail, and water the plants. If the card's image works its spell, the recipient usually wishes—just for a second or two—that he or she were out there on the highway too, taking it all in with those who have been good enough to write.

Most all of us know full well that the act of "getting there" remains an important part of any vacation or road adventure. This especially holds true for any trip on Route 66. The vacation officially begins the instant the tires roll onto the pavement. Unlike on impersonal interstates and monotonous turnpikes, nothing on Route 66 is cast in stone. Adventure and excitement lurk around every curve. At filling stations, curio shops, and motor courts, travelers share good stories and swap tips on roadside eateries. If you haven't visited a particular Route 66 cafe before, there is always the chance of contracting ptomaine poisoning or else finding the best plate of enchiladas, bowl of stew, or hamburger platter in the world.

The bottom line is this: Route 66 is worth writing home about. Here is your chance to do just that.

We have selected thirty of the best images from our personal Route 66 postcard collection for you to enjoy and, we hope, use when you journey down the Mother Road. All you need is a pencil or a pen and some stamps.

Enjoy the trip! And don't forget to write!

Suzanne Fitzgerald Wallis
Michael Wallis

Michael and Suzanne Fitzgerald Wallis
Somewhere on Route 66

Chicago Art Institute, Michigan Boulevard, Chicago, Ill.

KAUFMANN-FABRY PHOTO

Chicago Art Institute
Route 66 Begins (or Ends) in Downtown Chicago, Not Far
from the Famed Art Institute

Post Card

First
Class
Stamp

From Route 66 Postcards. © 1993 Michael and Suzanne Wallis. St. Martin's Press.

*Wallis Collection/Originally published by
Colourpicture Publications.*

South Sixth Street Bridge, Springfield, Illinois
State Capital, Lincoln's Home and Final Resting Place
Proud Route 66 City

Post Card

From Route 66 Postcards. © 1993 Michael and Suzanne Wallis. St. Martin's Press.

First
Class
Stamp

*Wallis Collection/Curt Teich Postcard Archives,
Lake County (Illinois) Museum.*

BROADVIEW MOTOR COURT
U.S. 54, Junction By Pass 66
SPRINGFIELD, ILLINOIS

Broadview Motor Hotel

Phone 7638, Springfield, Illinois

Extra Fine—None Better—Rest in Best

Witt Workman, Owner

Post Card

From Route 66 Postcards. © 1993 Michael and Suzanne Wallis. St. Martin's Press.

First
Class
Stamp

Wallis Collection/Originally published by National Advertising.

GREETINGS from
AMERICA'S MAIN STREET
U.S. 66
Scenic MISSOURI
© CURT TEICH & CO., INC.

Scenic Missouri
Scenic U.S. 66 crosses Missouri, a distance of 300 miles between St. Louis and Joplin.

U—Scenic View in Meramec State Park, Sullivan • Main Street, Joplin

S—Abou Ben Adhem Shrine Mosque, Springfield • Big Piney River and Bluffs at Devil's Elbow

6—Scenic Bluffs along the Gasconade River • Post Headquarters, Fort Leonard Wood

6—Statue of Saint Louis, St. Louis • Along Scenic U.S. Highway 66 in the Ozarks

Post Card

From Route 66 Postcards. © 1993 Michael and Suzanne Wallis. St. Martin's Press.

First Class Stamp

Wallis Collection/Curt Teich Postcard Archives, Lake County (Illinois) Museum.

Chain of Rocks Bridge
The Most Popular Route 66 Crossing Over the Mighty
Mississippi

Post Card

From Route 66 Postcards. © 1993 Michael and Suzanne Wallis. St. Martin's Press.

First
Class
Stamp

*Wallis Collection/Originally published by Blair
Cedar and Novelty Works.*

PENNANT HOTEL

Rolla, Mo. (On U. S. Highways 66 and 63)

Complete hotel and restaurant accommodations of the highest type, designed especially for motorists. Service and facilities unexcelled in metropolitan areas.

Pennant Hotel

Pennant Hotel and Tavern, located near the Ozark Mountain country, is the answer to America's demand for comfort and convenience on the highway. These facilities are far ahead of anything else by the roadside and excel the average accommodations of first-class establishments in larger cities.

Post Card

From Route 66 Postcards. © 1993 Michael and Suzanne Wallis. St. Martin's Press.

First Class Stamp

Wallis Collection/Originally published by Standard Printing Company.

← TO ST.LOUIS   U.S. 66 BY-PASS TO JOPLIN—TULSA—OKLA.CITY →

U.S. 65 & 66

S.166
S.66

U.S. 65

Rock Village Court

SPRINGFIELD   MISSOURI

**Intersection Hi-Ways U. S. 66, 65 and 166
On U. S. 66, Follow By-Pass**

*Hotel
Facilities*

*Coffee
Shop*

MEMBER
UNITED
MOTOR COURTS

Rock Village Court

Springfield, Missouri • In City Limits at NE Edge •
Gateway to the Ozarks • An unusually picturesque
group of quarried native stone and glass brick cottages
and hotel. Ultra Modern, Automatic Fire Protection.
Private Telephones, PBX. Mail and Telegraph Service.
Steam Heat. Free Radios. Air Cooled. Tiled Combination
Tub and Shower Baths. Coffee Shop Serving Excellent
Foods. Phone: 1332. P.O. Box 1651 SS.

Post Card

From Route 66 Postcards. © 1993 Michael and Suzanne Wallis. St. Martin's Press.

First
Class
Stamp

*Wallis Collection/Originally published by MWM
Color-Litho.*

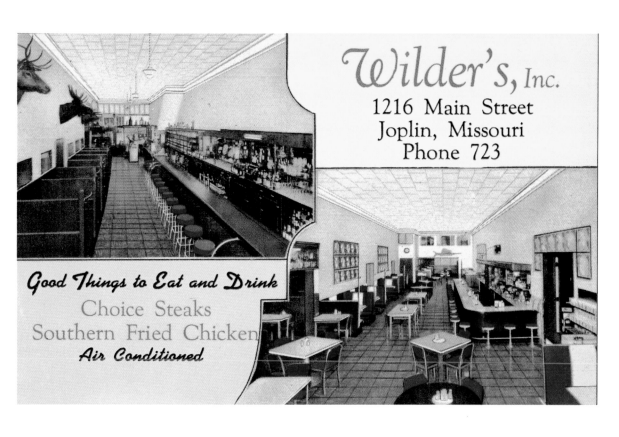

Wilder's, Inc.
1216 Main Street
Joplin, Missouri
Phone 723

Good Things to Eat and Drink
Choice Steaks
Southern Fried Chicken
Air Conditioned

Wilder's

Excellent Food and Bar Service • From 6 AM until 1:30 AM • Information to Tourists • Latest Sports Returns • Located at Joplin, Missouri, in the Heart of the Ozark Mountains

Post Card

From Route 66 Postcards, © 1993 Michael and Suzanne Wallis. St. Martin's Press.

Wallis Collection/Curt Teich Postcard Archives, Lake County (Illinois) Museum.

Ben Stanley's
CAFE
Nationally Famous
STEAKS
CHICKEN
SEA FOOD
One Mile South of
MIAMI, OKLA.
on Hi-way 66

Ben Stanley's Cafe
Steaks—Chicken—Sea Food…Nationally Famous
"We Don't Fool You, We Feed You."

Post Card

First
Class
Stamp

From Route 66 Postcards. © 1993 Michael and Suzanne Wallis. St. Martin's Press.

Wallis Collection/Originally published by MWM Color-Litho.

DEDICATED TO WILL ROGERS, THE WORLD'S GREATEST HUMORIST, CLAREMORE, OKLA., U.S.A.

Hotel Will Rogers

Featuring "That Eastern Atmosphere, Western Welcome and Southern Hospitality." • Just after the dedication, February 7, 1930, Will Rogers said, regarding his hotel, "I was more proud to see my name in electric lights in my old home town on an institution built for service to the public, than I ever was on the biggest theatre on Broadway."

Post Card

From Route 66 Postcards. © 1993 Michael and Suzanne Wallis. St. Martin's Press.

First Class Stamp

Wallis Collection/Originally published by Tichnor Bros., Inc.

Woman with Two Alligators

A.R.K. Animal Reptile Kingdom • Catoosa Alligator Ranch, Rt. 1, Box 4, Catoosa, Oklahoma 74015, U.S. Hy. 66 • Nature wonders of interest for any age • Advance bookings for children's birthday parties in the ARK • Cameras Welcome • Owned and operated by Hugh and Zelta Davis • Over 40 years experience in zoological work.

Post Card

From Route 66 Postcards. © 1993 Michael and Suzanne Wallis. St. Martin's Press.

First Class Stamp

Wallis Collection/Originally published by Gough Photo Service.

Tulsa Sky Line
Where Route 66 Uses 11th Street as Its Alias

Post Card

From Route 66 Postcards. © 1993 Michael and Suzanne Wallis. St. Martin's Press.

First
Class
Stamp

*Wallis Collection/Curt Teich Postcard Archives,
Lake County (Illinois) Museum.*

PARK-O-TELL

FIREPROOF

OKLAHOMA CITY, OKLA.

2 Blocks North of State Capitol Bldg.

ON U. S. HIGHWAYS
Nos. 77 and 66

1375-30

Park-O-Tell

You can drive right in the Park-O-Tell
100 car garage, under the same roof.
As Spick and Span as Next Year!

Post Card

First
Class
Stamp

From Route 66 Postcards. © 1993 Michael and Suzanne Wallis. St. Martin's Press.

*Wallis Collection/Curt Teich Postcard Archives,
Lake County (Illinois) Museum.*

Greetings from WILL ROGERS FIELD
OKLAHOMA

Will Rogers Field
During WWII Route 66 Was Filled With Troops Going
to Battle

Post Card

First
Class
Stamp

From Route 66 Postcards. © 1993 Michael and Suzanne Wallis. St. Martin's Press.

Wallis Collection/Curt Teich Postcard Archives,
Lake County (Illinois) Museum.

Motel Conway

Refrigerated Air-Conditioned, Steam Heat, Brick Construction, Tile Showers, Children's Playground, Free TV in Rooms, Filling Station and Good Food Next Door.
• Reservation until 6 PM Without Deposit • Indian Curio Shop • Drive-In Theatre 5 Blocks • On Highway 66 and 270, West El Reno, Oklahoma Phone: An 2-0261

Post Card

From Route 66 Postcards. © 1993 Michael and Suzanne Wallis. St. Martin's Press.

First Class Stamp

Wallis Collection/Curt Teich Postcard Archives, Lake County (Illinois) Museum.

SHAMROCK, TEXAS

ENTRANCE CITY
TO TEXAS
ON U. S. 66

First Baptist Church

UNITED STATES POST OFFICE
SHAMROCK TEXAS

U. S. POST OFFICE

SHAMROCK

GENERAL
HOSPITAL

HOSPITAL

© MC C. CO.

Shamrock, Texas
The Panhandle Town Where Everyone Is Irish

Post Card

From Route 66 Postcards. © 1993 Michael and Suzanne Wallis. St. Martin's Press.

First
Class
Stamp

*Wallis Collection/Curt Teich Postcard Archives,
Lake County (Illinois) Museum.*

MC C. CO. PHOTO 72107

8B-H70

LONG CHAMP DINING SALON — EAST OF CITY ON HIGHWAY 60 & 66 — AMARILLO, TEXAS

Long Champ Dining Salon
705 N.E. 8th Ave., Amarillo, Texas (Pop. 80,000)
Nation-wide reputation of the finest eating place
from coast to coast, specializing in sea foods.
"Where the Plains Meet the Sea."

Post Card

From Route 66 Postcards. © 1993 Michael and Suzanne Wallis. St. Martin's Press.

First
Class
Stamp

*Wallis Collection/Curt Teich Postcard Archives,
Lake County (Illinois) Museum.*

The Largest Longhorn Steer Alive
With Horns Measuring 6 feet Tip to Tip
Shown in Native Corral at the
New Mexico Museum of The Old West
On Highway 66

The famous
Longhorn Cattle
OF THE OLD WEST
are found today
only
on Govt. Reservations,
or in private ownership.

A Real Longhorn

Longhorn Ranch on Route 66.
New Mexico Museum of the Old West, 48 miles east of
Albuquerque and 70 miles west of Santa Rosa, New
Mexico.

Post Card

From Route 66 Postcards. © 1993 Michael and Suzanne Wallis. St. Martin's Press.

First
Class
Stamp

*Wallis Collection/Originally published by Alfred
McGarr Advertising Service.*

Sandia Mountains

Highway U.S. 66 through Sandia Mountains east of
Albuquerque, New Mexico • The highway winds through
the scenic Sandia (Watermelon) Mountains towards the
city which nestles in the foothills just beyond the peaks in
the background. Picturesque little Spanish villages dot the
landscape at frequent intervals, adding interest to the
scene.

Post Card

From Route 66 Postcards. © 1993 Michael and Suzanne Wallis. St. Martin's Press.

First
Class
Stamp

Wallis Collection/Curt Teich Postcard Archives,
Lake County (Illinois) Museum.

OKLAHOMA JOE'S   Albuquerque, N. Mex.

Ladies and Men's Rest Rooms   Where Tourists Meet

Oklahoma Joe's

Dixie Genuine Pit Bar-B-Que • 1720 East Central Avenue on Highway 66, Albuquerque, New Mexico • Breakfast, Lunch, Dinner and Sandwiches at Moderate Prices • We BAR-B-QUE the Old Fashion Way, Ribs, Beef, Pork, Chicken. All food supervised by Oklahoma Joe in person, Proprietor. For information stop at Oklahoma Joe's.

Post Card

First Class Stamp

From Route 66 Postcards. © 1993 Michael and Suzanne Wallis. St. Martin's Press.

Wallis Collection/Originally published by MWM Color-Litho.

Kimo Theatre

America's Foremost Indian Theatre, Albuquerque, New Mexico • The Kimo Theatre Building expresses architecturally, in its composite design, the traditions of New Mexico and the old Southwest. One of the few typically American Indian architectural expressions, with a suggestion of the Spanish in its contours, this unusual edifice, both inside and out, provides an atmosphere of historical romance unequalled elsewhere in America.

Post Card

From Route 66 Postcards. © 1993 Michael and Suzanne Wallis, St. Martin's Press.

Wallis Collection/Curt Teich Postcard Archives, Lake County (Illinois) Museum.

First
Class
Stamp

MAISEL'S · INDIAN · TRADING · POST ·

MAISEL'S

MAISEL'S INDIAN TRADING POST — 510 W. Central Ave. — ALBUQUERQUE, NEW MEXICO

1B-H368

Maisel's Indian Trading Post

510 Central Ave., Albuquerque, New Mexico
Show windows and murals of the most unusual building
in the Southwest • Fresco murals by famous Indian
painters • Turquoise and petrified wood terrazzo inlaid
with over 200 Mexican pesos • More than 50 Indian
silversmiths and a number of turquoise cutters can be
seen applying their craft • The largest and most
complete collection of Indian and Mexican handicraft
in the world is on display • Makers of genuine coin
silver and turquoise jewelry

Post Card

From Route 66 Postcards. © 1993 Michael and Suzanne Wallis. St. Martin's Press.

First
Class
Stamp

*Wallis Collection/Curt Teich Postcard Archives,
Lake County (Illinois) Museum.*

WIGWAM
VILLAGE No. 6
800 W. HOPI DRIVE
PHONE 310

U. S. 66 （77） U. S. 260

HOLBROOK, ARIZONA

Sleep in a Wigwam

A novel and unique place to stay in the heart of Indian country. Gateway to Petrified Forest and Painted Desert National Monuments. Solid hickory furniture. Modern throughout. Insulated for your peace and quiet.

Post Card

From Route 66 Postcards. © 1993 Michael and Suzanne Wallis. St. Martin's Press.

First Class Stamp

Wallis Collection/Curt Teich Postcard Archives, Lake County (Illinois) Museum.

Hopi Indians (Orlin and Zellah) on the Edge of Painted Desert

Hopi Indians

Arizona's Famous Painted Desert on Route 66—Where
the Soil and Rocks Are Tinted Blue, Chocolate, Purple,
Rose, and Vermillion.

Post Card

From Route 66 Postcards. © 1993 Michael and Suzanne Wallis, St. Martin's Press.

First
Class
Stamp

Wallis Collection/Originally published by
Colourpicture Publications.

METEOR CRATER ~ ~ ~ 4150 FT. WIDE ~ 600 FT. DEEP

VIEW OF METEOR CRATER FROM HIGHWAY AT METEOR ARIZ. ~ ON U.S. 66

Meteor Crater

This crater was formed many thousands of years ago by the falling of an immense meteor, estimated to weigh 5,000,000 tons. The crater marking its crash into the earth is 600 feet deep and 4,150 feet across from rim to rim.

Post Card

From Route 66 Postcards. © 1993 Michael and Suzanne Wallis. St. Martin's Press.

First
Class
Stamp

Wallis Collection/Originally published by Herz Post Cards.

Williams Motel

"The Gateway to Grand Canyon"
U.S. 66 - 89, Williams, Arizona

Williams Motel

Phone: 228. A new, 16 unit, elegantly furnished motel with thermostatically controlled heat. Tubs and full-tile showers. Carpeted wall-to-wall. Dorothy & Dick Boyack, Owners

Post Card

First Class Stamp

From Route 66 Postcards. © 1993 Michael and Suzanne Wallis. St. Martin's Press.

Wallis Collection/Originally published by Colourpicture Publications.

Oranges and Snow Capped Mountains

Sunny California—at the End of the Mother Road—
Beckons. The Land of Milk and Honey for Dust Bowl
Migrants and Weary Pilgrims.

Post Card

First
Class
Stamp

From Route 66 Postcards. © 1993 Michael and Suzanne Wallis. St. Martin's Press.

*Wallis Collection/Curt Teich Postcard Archives,
Lake County (Illinois) Museum.*

San Bernardino Polytechnic High School, San Bernardino, California.

Polytechnic High School
Beautiful San Bernardino, California—The City
Founded by Mormons Sixty Miles East of L.A.

Post Card

From Route 66 Postcards. © 1993 Michael and Suzanne Wallis. St. Martin's Press.

First
Class
Stamp

Wallis Collection/Curt Teich Postcard Archives,
Lake County (Illinois) Museum.

L.A. 199

Greetings from LOS ANGELES

CALIFORNIA

© C. T. & CO.

6A-H1000

Greetings from Los Angeles
City of Angels

Post Card

From Route 66 Postcards. © 1993 Michael and Suzanne Wallis. St. Martin's Press.

First
Class
Stamp

*Wallis Collection/Curt Teich Postcard Archives,
Lake County (Illinois) Museum.*

Palisades Park
Where Santa Monica Boulevard Meets Ocean Avenue and
Route 66 Ends (or Begins)

Post Card

First
Class
Stamp

From Route 66 Postcards. © 1993 Michael and Suzanne Wallis. St. Martin's Press.

*Wallis Collection/Originally published by
Longshaw Card Co.*